TO DO LI

S

- ☐ COLIN XMAS CA
- ☐ Buy family & friend
- ☐ Buy eco wrapping paper
- ☐ organise clients xmas slots

SCUBA EQUIPMENT

DIVE TRIP excl Nitrox.
BOAT
FLIGHTS
VISA £30
HOTEL?
NITROX

Always jingle all the way.
No one likes a half-assed jiggler.

A little more sparkle and a
little less stress,
This christmas and New Year
I wish you the very best.

It's be-gin-ing to look a
lot like christmas.

15865931R00079

Printed in Great Britain
by Amazon